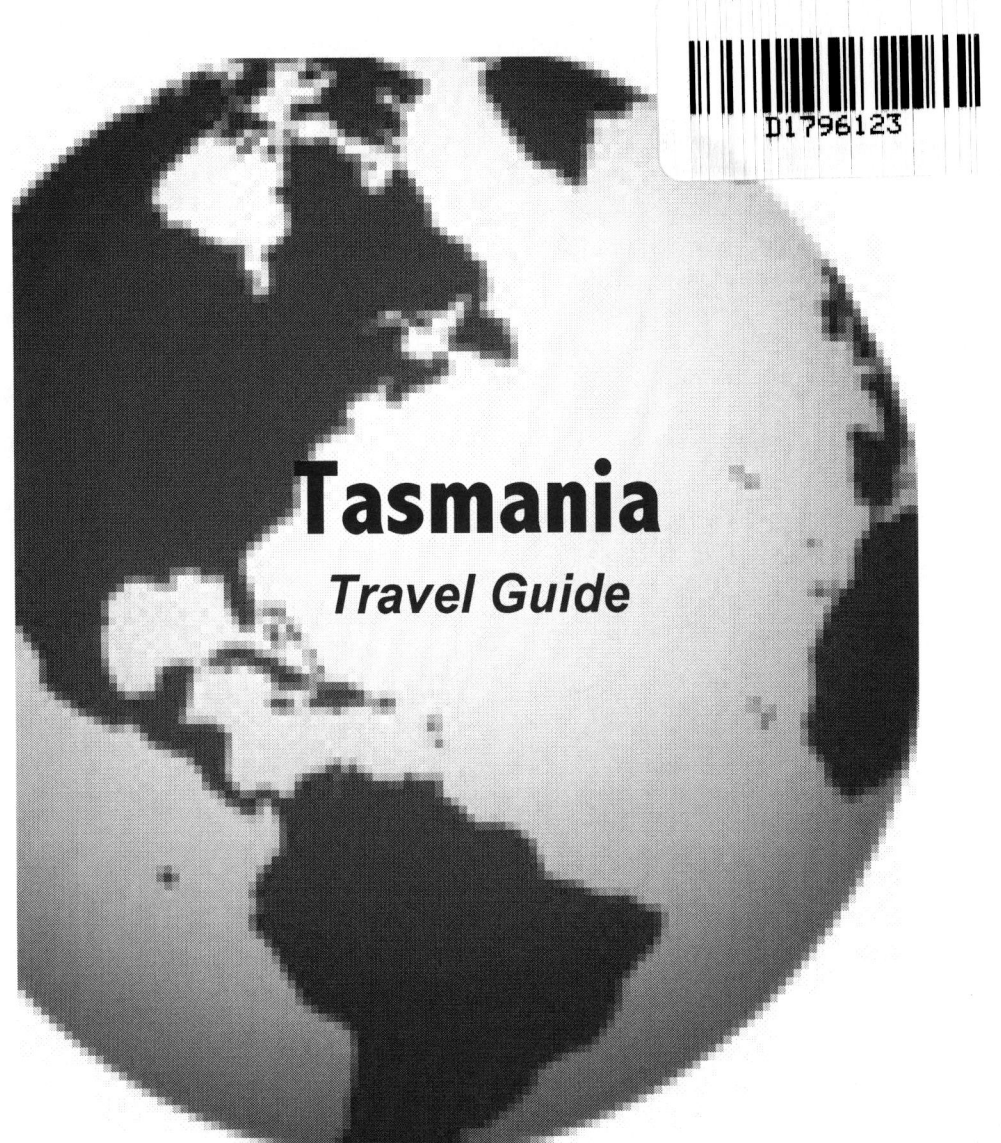

Tasmania
Travel Guide

Quick Trips Series

Table of Contents

Tasmania

Tasmania is the smallest and only island state in Australia with nearly half of its archipelago of 334 islands being protected. Tasmania's national parks and UNESCO World Heritage sites make the state a popular destination for tourists.

TASMANIA TRAVEL GUIDE

Tasmania lies to the south of the state of Victoria across the Bass Strait and was discovered in the mid 17th century by the Dutch explorer, Abel Tasman. Although Abel initially named the island after his sponsor – Anthony van Diemen; the island was officially renamed by the British to Tasmania in 1856. Wild at heart and beauty, Tasmania is promoted to the visitors as 'A World Apart, Not A World Away'. This natural state is also known as 'The Island of Inspiration'.

Tasmania, with large areas of dolerite (surges of magma in volcanic zones), has a stunningly beautiful landscape with lots of colourful wildlife. The island is divided into a number of regions. The most populous region is Southern Tasmania with the capital and 2nd oldest Australian city – Hobart. The region also includes the picturesque Port

TASMANIA TRAVEL GUIDE

Arthur. Northern Tasmania is more mountainous and is home to the popular Tamar Valley. The North West Coast region has a few coastal towns but is more popular for the scenic inland areas. The South West Coast region is a nature lover's delight with the whole area protected as a national park. Whereas the East Coast region is visited for the stunning beaches, the West Coast has the historic mining centers. Tasmania also has two extremely scenic islands in its Bass Strait Islands region.

Tasmania has something to offer for everyone. From basking in the sun in one of its stunning beaches and taking a guided nocturnal penguin-watching tour, to walking through the heritage national parks and enjoying the locally made wines and ciders, Tasmania is truly a world apart.

🌏 Customs & Culture

Tasmania is inhabited by about half a million people and there are more than a dozen annual events that keep the cultural calendar full. The summer month of January has the Cygnet Folk Festival. During this festival in Port Cygnet in the 2nd weekend of January, various performances and exhibitions on art, dance, and music are held in different venues across town.

The MONA Festival of Art and Music in January is a celebration of art and sound through theatre, dance, and visual art. The winter version of this festival – held in June – is called the Dark MOFO. February and March has the Australian Wooden Boat festival in Hobart, and the MS Fest music festival in Launceston.

TASMANIA TRAVEL GUIDE

The winter months have a number of festivals and events including the 6-day Targa Tasmania Road Rally. The popular agricultural festival of Agfest - http://www.agfest.com.au/ - is a celebration of the farming and produce of the land. Originally held in the mainland, the fest is now an important part of the Tasmanian calendar. A major multi-art form festival – Ten Days on the Island - http://www.tendays.org.au/ is held all over the state with a 100 venues and over 250 individual events. Music lovers can enjoy the Antarctic Midwinter festival and the Davenport Jazz festival in June and July. Similar to the Agfest, the Royal Launceston Show and the Royal Hobart Show celebrate the rural exploits of Tasmania. Fun events like livestock judging and wood chopping along with plenty of food and games stalls keep the whole family amused. Food lovers can also attend the Taste of

Tasmania - http://www.thetasteoftasmania.com.au/ at the Salamanca Market and the waterfront area during Christmas. This weeklong festival is the largest food and wine festival on the island and is attended by nearly half a million visitors – the same as the population of the island!

Classical music lovers can attend a performance of the Tasmanian Symphony Orchestra at the Federation Concert hall. The island also has a number of small bands and individual artists who perform classical music at various venues across town. At the other extreme, one can attend jigs by metal-bands like the renowned Tasmanian Psycroptic or Striborg.

Not handicapped by its geographic size, Tasmania has a strong literary culture. In the early days, the island is found as a subject of writings of many discoverers and explorers. The landscape and the lives of the Aboriginal people provided inspiration to those writers. Over the years, Tasmania became home to many authors and there is a growing interest in literature on the island. The government promotes literature through many art festivals and book launches throughout the year.

Sport is a popular pastime of the island state and there are a variety of sporting events to choose from. Hobart is a popular international venue for cricket and features many important matches of the state and national team. The Aurora Stadium is home to the Australian Rules Football, a very popular sport in this part of the world. The 5-day Sydney to Hobart Yacht Race that starts on Boxing Day is not just a local event but a major tourist attraction.

Soccer and tennis are 2 other popular sports that is closely followed and played in Tasmania.

🌏 Geography

The island of Tasmania is located to the south of the Australian mainland, off the coast of the state of Victoria.

The closest major mainland city is Melbourne. Separated by the Bass Strait, it is connected regularly by ferry services from the mainland.

Tasmania is served by 2 airports – the Hobart International Airport (IATA: HBA) - http://www.hobartairport.com.au/ and the Launceston Airport (IATA: LST) - http://www.launcestonairport.com.au/. These are 2 of the fastest growing airports in the country and although they do not have a regular schedule of international flights they have all the facilities and amenities of international terminals. These airports are also very important for their location; connecting the country with the continent of Antarctica. A recent growth in the services of low-cost airlines has seen a sharp rise in the passenger count in both these airports. Hobart airport has shuttle buses that operate to and from the city for every flight. It is run by Redline - http://www.tasredline.com.au/. Taxis and rental cars are also available. Launceston Airport also has a shuttle service (Tel: 03 6343 66 77) connecting the airport to the town in a 15-minute commute costing $18 (Australian dollar). The usual taxi and rental car service is also available.

TASMANIA TRAVEL GUIDE

A popular and common way to reach Tasmania from the mainland is through the ferry. The Spirit of Tasmania - http://www.spiritoftasmania.com.au/ runs regular ferry services connecting Melbourne and Devonport – the 3rd largest city in Tasmania.

Ferries usually start the journey around 8:00 pm and reach port next day at 7:00 am, both ways. Services are increased during peak seasons. These fully equipped ferries can even carry private vehicles. An adult ticket for the one way trip costs between $120 and $180. A car can be transferred for as low as $65 and bicycles for $7.

Once on the island, the best way to move around is with a private vehicle as the tourist pockets are spread all over the island. There are a number of car rental companies to choose from – Hertz -

https://www.hertz.com.au/rentacar/reservation/, Avis -

http://www.avis.com.au, and Sixt -

https://www.redspot.com.au/. For those planning to drive,

it has to be kept in mind that Australia has a left-lane

driving rule. Speed limits are 110 km per hr for highways

and 50 km per hr for built-up areas. Speed limits are

strictly enforced and driving even 5 km above the speed

limit will incur a fine. To drive in Australia, one must be 21

years of age and have an International Driver's License in

English. While driving in Tasmania, especially through the

inland highways, it is difficult to drive at the maximum

speed limit because of the curves, strong winds, and poor

road conditions. It is advisable to always keep some

buffer when calculating the driving time. Cars can be

brought from the mainland on the ferry.

For those opting for public transport can use the bus service run by Redline Tasmania - http://www.tasredline.com.au/, and Tassielink - http://www.tassielink.com.au/. Intra-city bus service is run by Metro Tasmania - http://www.metrotas.com.au/, and Merseylink - http://www.merseylink.com.au/.

However, it is to be kept in mind that bus services are not very frequent and could often be a long wait; the journey could also be tedious, for the distance and road conditions.

🌏 Weather & Best Time to Visit

Tasmania experiences a cool temperate climate with summer between December and February when the average high is around 21 degrees Celsius and the average low around 12 degrees. Autumn months of March, April, and May see the climate getting cooler and wetter as winter settles in. Winter between June and August is cold and wet. The average high is around 12 degrees and low around 5 degrees. However, being a mountainous region, certain inland areas of high altitude can get colder and receive snowfall. Spring – between September and November – sees a transition from the cold and wet weather to considerably drier and warmer climate. The spring and summer months draw the maximum number of tourists to the island because of the warm and dry weather.

Sights & Activities: What to See & Do

Hobart

Located at the foot of the stunningly majestic Mt

Wellington, Hobart is the smallest capital city of Australia

and one of the most historic. Located in the south west of

the island, Hobart is the 2nd oldest (after Sydney) and the

coldest capital city of the island nation. In 2013, it was

listed by Lonely Planet as one of the Top 10 Best in Travel cities in the world. With a great mix of history, culture, and art, Hobart is one of the most popular tourist destinations in Tasmania.

For those flying into the Hobart International Airport can take the shuttle to reach the city centre. The one-way trip costs $15. It is recommended to book tickets online at http://www.tasredline.com.au/ to avoid any delays at the airport. Taxis (approximately $45) and rental cars are also available. There is no public bus service from the airport with the closest bus route at a distance of about 5 km from the airport. Within the city, one can use the public bus service. The day ticket ($4.80) is recommended. The bus travels to most of the tourist attractions which can then be covered by foot. As the city limits are not too far, cycling is also a popular option.

Founded in 1804 as a penal colony along the banks of the River Derwent, Hobart today has many tourist attractions to choose from. A walk along the old streets will take past many beautiful Victorian and Georgian architecture. A short trip out of town takes one to many of the wineries of Hobart – there are even wine tours to choose from.

Salamanca Place & Market

Located in Sullivans Cove, Salamanca Place is a precinct in Hobart that is popular for the Saturday Market, and dozens of restaurants, galleries, pubs, and craft shops. The place is lined with rows of mid 19th century Georgian sandstone warehouses that now house many of the shops and eateries. Named after the Spanish town of the same name, Salamanca is the most vibrant part of Hobart and a must-visit if one is in town.

Every Saturday, the Salamanca Market (8:30 am to 3:00 pm) takes over the square. A visit to the market is a priority if one is in Hobart over the weekend. From clothes to accessories, and from local produce to unique handmade crafts, the Salamanca Market has it all. A perfect place to sit and watch people or have a relaxing glass of local wine after a bout of shopping, Salamanca scores high for all tourists visiting the island capital.

Royal Tasmanian Botanical Gardens

Located on a site that was once used by the Aboriginal people, the Botanical Gardens is an important conservation centre for plants and trees in Hobart. It was founded in 1818 and is home to a large collection of historic plants and trees, some well over a century old. The Gardens has the only Subantarctic Plant House in the world. The plants for this House have been collected from the heritage-listed Macquarie Island near Antarctica. Other than many exhibition sites, the Gardens also have a restaurant and a souvenir shop. Located near the Queens Domain, about 2 km from the Hobart CBD, the Wi-Fi enabled Botanical Gardens is open 7 days a week throughout the year. Entry to the Gardens is free;

donation boxes are placed at various places in the Gardens for those who want to contribute.

Tasmanian Museum & Art Gallery

Established in 1843, the Tasmanian Museum & Art Gallery - http://www.tmag.tas.gov.au is the oldest 'Royal Society' outside England.

With some unique collections in geology, photography, historic coins, and decorative art, the museum attracts over 300000 visitors every year. Over the years the TMAG has established itself as a combination of museum, gallery, and herbarium; the largest of its kind in the country. There are a number of interesting and eye-catching permanent and floating exhibitions throughout the year. Located at Dunn Place, the TMAG is open from 10:00 am to 5:00 pm every day except Anzac day, Christmas Day, and Good Friday.

Other popular museums in Hobart include the Maritime Museum of Tasmania and the Museum of Old and New Art.

The city of Hobart has a number of other attractions in and around town. A hike or a drive to Mt Wellington enables guests to have a bird's eye-view of the city and its surroundings. Details of the weather conditions and access routes can be found at - http://www.wellingtonpark.org.au/. The Peppermint Bay - http://www.peppermintbay.com.au/, Cascade Brewery - http://www.cascadebreweryco.com.au/, Shot Tower,

Cadbury's Chocolate Factory, and a number of winery tours are popular crowd pullers in town.

Hobart is also a place of culinary delight with its great wineries and fresh seafood and produce. Even if one cannot visit the wineries in the Coal River Valley or Huon Valley region, the city itself has many great places to savor the best in food and drinks.

🌏 Launceston

The city of Launceston is the 2nd largest city in the island of Tasmania. Founded in 1805, it is one of the oldest cities in the country, and like many other Australian cities, it is named after a British town, Launceston in Cornwall. Launceston (Australia) has many historic sites and buildings along with natural wonders in and around town that attract many visitors throughout the year. Just like the island capital Hobart, Launceston is also growing in to a major tourist centre in Tasmania. The small city attracts over half a million visitors annually with nearly a quarter of them coming from the UK.

Launceston has its own small airport - http://www.launcestonairport.com.au/ that has daily connections with Melbourne and Sydney. It is connected with Hobart and Devonport Port City through Highway 1. Once in Launceston, it is best use a rental car as public bus service is few and infrequent. Cycling is also a great option to move around town. However, most of the city attractions are within walking distance.

Cataract Gorge

Barely a 15-minute walk from the city centre along the River Tamar, this river gorge is a unique natural phenomenon in an urban setting. Once in the gorge, one can follow the pathway that was built in the late 19th century. This pathway – the King's Bridge-Cataract Walk - along the face of the cliff looks down onto the picturesque South Esk River.

The south side of the basin – called the First Basin - has an open area and a swimming pool. The area is surrounded by a bushland adjacent to the Launceston Beach. The contrasting north side – called the Cliff Grounds – is shadier and has a Victorian Garden with exotic plants and ferns. The 1972-chairlift across the river is the longest single-span chairlift in the world.

The Gorge is an ideal place for the whole family. This wild urban reserve has many interesting walks and trails that are perfect for a hike on a sunny day. A kiosk, restaurant, and rolling lawns provide ample opportunities for relaxation. One can also see peacocks and wallabies in the park area. Another interesting feature is the Duck Reach Power Station upstream. Commissioned in 1893, it was lighting Launceston by 1895 making it the first Australian city to be lit by hydro-electricity.

Queen Victoria Museum & Art Gallery (QVMAG)

The QVMAG http://www.qvmag.tas.gov.au was founded in 1891 and stands today as the largest museum outside a capital city in Australia. Located at 2 different sites –

Royal Park and old Launceston Railway Workshops - within the city of Launceston, the museum has an excellent collection on colonial and contemporary Tasmanian art, natural sciences, history, and zoology. The QVMAG is basically divided into 3 sections, the museum, an art gallery, and a planetarium.

Exhibitions in the museum section include preserved railway workshops, the Sydney Cove shipwreck, and models of dinosaurs and death masks. The art gallery section has a number of exhibitions, some accompanied with guided tours. The planetarium was established in 1968 and now has enhanced viewing facilities with digital features after its renovation. The QVMAG also hosts many interactive events for children and adults throughout the year. The premise has a museum shop and a café.

TASMANIA TRAVEL GUIDE

The QVMAG is open from 10:00 am to 4:00 pm every day (except Christmas Day and Good Friday). It has free entry.

Launceston offers a number of other attractions to its visitors. The City Park and historic streets are ideal for a relaxing stroll. The cruise or visits to the wineries of the Tamar Valley region are popular getaways for the locals and visitors alike. Launceston is a base to explore north Tasmania. Popular destination from the city includes the Tamar Island Wetlands, historic George Town, the coastal town of St Helens, the lavender farm of Scottsdale, and the Ben Lomond National Park.

◉ Historic Convict Sites

An important and defining part of Tasmania is its convict history. When the British and Irish prisons were getting overcrowded in the late 18th century, many of the convicts were shipped to Australia. In July 2010, UNESCO listed 11 Australian former convict sites in its World Heritage List, 5 of which are in Tasmania.

Port Arthur Site

The historic convict site at Port Arthur - http://www.portarthur.org.au is the best known site from the convict era. Located on the south side of the Tasman Peninsula, the site was originally a timber-getting station before it was transformed into a penal colony for secondary offenders. The colony, operative between 1833 and 1877, was known for the arduous labour and strong surveillance. Prisoners were engaged in sandstone quarries and timber felling.

Spread over 136 hectares in a picturesque landscape, one can see more than 30 of the convict-built structures and some ruins. The site, along with the gardens and the ruins are open from 8:30 am until sunset. There are different categories of package passes available for the entry (single day, 2 days, or late afternoon), guided tour, harbor cruise, and meals. There is no ticket for only an entry to the site.

Estates of Brickendon & Woolmers

Operative between the 1820s and the 1850s in the 2 neighbouring estates in north Tasmania, the convicts in this penal colony were assigned to private masters and were made to work on the farming fields. The male convicts were engaged as gardeners, agricultural hands, and blacksmiths, while the women were engaged as domestic maids.

The convicts were given food and clothing in exchange of their labour. The 'masters' were also responsible for the health and wellbeing of the convicts. Brickendon Estate is open between 9:30 am and 5:00 pm from Tuesday to Sunday; Woolmers Estate is open from 10:00 am to 4:30 pm every day with extended hours in summer.

Darlington Probation Station

This penal station (1825-32 & 1842-50) was located in the Maria Island National Park near the east coast. This all-male station used to categorize convicts based on their crime and subsequent behavior. The Darlington Station is the best preserved amongst the convict sites in Tasmania with 14 convict buildings and ruins spread over 361 hectares. The visiting hours are in sync with the Park's opening hours.

Coal Mines Site

Located in the Little Norfolk Bay in the north of the Tasman Peninsula, this penal colony was operational between 1833 and 1848. The prisoners were made to work in the coalmines that subsequently contributed to the development of the colony. The station was known for its severe workload and punishment. The site, spread over 214 hectares, has more than two dozen convict buildings, accommodations, and cells.

Cascades Female Factory

This all-female convict station was located in a valley at the base of Mt Wellington in Hobart. The convicts were categorized based on their crime and assigned jobs accordingly. The station had many buildings including a hospital, cookhouses, workshops, church, and solitary cells. 3 of the 5 original yards along with some administrative buildings are still intact and open to the public between Monday and Friday from 9:00 am to 5:00 pm.

🌐 East Coach Beach Resorts

The east coast of Tasmania is home to not only some of the best wineries of the island but also to the best beaches of Tasmania. There are multiple award winning beach houses and eco-lodges that are lined on the pristine white beaches that open up to the beautiful turquoise waters. There are a number beaches, bays, and towns that attract thousands of tourists every year to this picturesque part of the island.

Bay of Fires

One of the most visited attractions in the east coast is the Bay of Fires. The bay got its name in 1773 from the fires lit by the native Aboriginal people that were sighted by Captain Tobias of the HMS Adventure, a part of the fleet of Captain Cook.

The bay extends from the Binalong Bay to the Edison Point and has a long stretch of white sand beaches, blue waters, and orange-coloured rocks. The northern part of the bay can be accessed through the Mount William

National Park. The southern part is designated as a conservation area. The bay has many facilities for camping, fishing, swimming, and boating.

Bicheno

Located 185 km north east of Hobart, the town of Bicheno is a popular beach resort and a fishing port. The town is easily accessible by road as it is just off the Tasman Highway. The mild climate of Bicheno makes it an ideal place for not only a beach outing, but also fishing of almost every type. Cray-fishing is, in fact, the largest industry in this town. The town can be easily covered by foot and one of the best walks is from the Diamond Island to the 'blowhole'. Another stunning attraction is the abundance of penguins. Although there are regular guided tours of the penguin colonies, one may come across penguins in and around the beach areas.

St. Helens

Located on the Georges Bay, St Helens is the largest town in north east Tasmania. Located about a 2-hr drive from the Launceston Airport, St Helens is becoming an increasingly popular tourist town with its white beaches, crystal clear waters, and orange lichen-covered rocks.

Other than enjoying the beach activities and the spectacular coastal scenery, one can visit the Mt William National Park for the famous 'kangaroo drive'.

Swansea

Located about a 90-minite drive from Hobart, the town of Swansea is near the Great Oyster Bay. Other than the beaches, the town has many historic buildings including the operating century-old Morris' General Store. There are many points for swimming and surfing. Lake Leake is popular for trout fishing whereas Mayfield Beach is visited for beach and rock fishing. The scenic Meetus Falls and Lost Falls are located close to the Lake Leake. Wine lovers can also visit the vineyards in Springvale and Craige Knowe.

Other popular regions in the east coast include the Coles Bay, Maria Island, Freycinet National Park, Orford, and Pyengana.

🌏 Bruny Island

Located off the south east coast of Tasmania, Bruny Island is home to some stunning natural landscape, boutique accommodation, and unforgettable culinary delight, providing the visitor with the ultimate wilderness experience. The popular Bruny Island Cruises - http://www.brunycruises.com.au/ was named as one of the top 100 experiences by Travel and Leisure magazine.

Bruny Island is best connected from Hobart. One can fly in as the island has a small landing strip but the most popular and cheap way is to cross the D'Entrecasteaux Bay that separates the island from the Tasmanian mainland. There are ferry connections from Hobart (The Meerambeena from Kettering port) and Melbourne (The Spirit of Tasmania). Once in Bruny Island, one can use a car for travelling although many of the attractions are best seen by foot.

The island has a number of townships including Adventure Bay, Lunawanna, Barnes Bay, Simpsons Bay, Alonnah, and Dennes Point.

The island is home to the Bruny Island National Park which has a number of walking trails and bushwalks. The beach area of the island is an excellent place to spot fairy penguins, fur seals, and white wallabies. It also has many opportunities and facilities for bird watching. Bruny Island is home to Australia's southernmost vineyard as well as the southernmost licensed pub making it an ideal place for wine lovers. One can also enjoy handmade fudge, truffles, berries, and fresh oysters. The Bruny Island

Cheese Company is renowned for some highly-acclaimed cheese products.

The iconic 1838 Cape Bruny Lighthouse was the oldest continuous serving lighthouse of the country and is now a part of the National Park. History lovers can visit the Bligh Museum (Adventure Bay) and the Bruny History Room (Alonnah).

Although popular as a day trip destination, Bruny Island has many facilities for accommodation at Adventure Bay and Dennes Point.

🌏 Cradle Mountain (Lake St Clair National Park)

Located about 50 km inland from the north east coast of Tasmania, the Cradle Mountain - Lake St Clair National

Park is part of Australia's World Heritage Wilderness Area. The Park is home to 1617m high Mt Ossa, the highest mountain of Tasmania. The Cradle Mountain area is one of the top tourist destinations on the island attracting nearly a quarter of the island visitors.

The Park was the brainchild of Gustav Weindorfer who bought some land in the area and built a chalet for his guests in 1912. By the 1930s, over 80 km of tracks were created along with guided tours on some of them. Over the years the tracks have been improved and extended. Today, there are many short and long walks in the Park that cover the major attractions like Cradle Mountain, Lake St Clair, and Dove Lake. Each walk comes with its own share of fascinating experience.

TASMANIA TRAVEL GUIDE

The popular short walks include the Dove Lake Loop Walk (approx 1 hr), Crater Lake Circuit (2 hrs), Cradle Mountain Summit (6 to 8 hrs), and the Enchanted Walk (20 min). Helicopter flights for a scenic tour is available, details of which can be found at the visitor centre of the Park. Flight tickets cost: Adult (2 seats) at $245 each, Child - $150.

There is a shuttle bus service available inside the Park but only for those who are not using a private vehicle. Vehicle pass (for up to an 8-seat vehicle) for 24hrs cost $24.

Entry fee for the overland track is separate and costs: Adult - $200; Child (under 17 years) - $150. There is a Holiday Pass that allows entry to any Tasmanian national park for 8 weeks. The Park area has many places for accommodation ranging from campsites to private cabins.

⊙ Hastings Caves

Located in the Huon Valley – about a 90-mnite drive from Hobart – the Hastings Caves is a natural phenomenon that both fascinates and relaxes the visitors. A part of the Hastings Caves State Reserve, it encompasses a stunning dolomite cave, a rich forest reserve, and a thermal pool with relaxing warm water. Part of the reserve is the dolomite Newdegate Cave that began forming millions of years ago and has a number of richly decorated natural chambers. It stands today as Australia's most visited tourist cave and one can enjoy the experience with expert commentaries from qualified tour guides from the Wildlife Service.

The entrance to the caves was found by timber workers in 1917. The Newdegate Cave is spacious and well lit and has a total of 214 stairs in different sets. The reflection of artificial light on the white and pink crystalline dolomite makes for a magical view. One should not forget to bring cold clothes as the temperature below is maintained at a constant 9 degrees Celsius.

The thermal pool is a place for the whole family. Located amidst the forest, the pool area is equipped with picnic spot, electric barbeques, showers, and shelters. The pool water is a constant 28 degrees Celsius and is hygienically controlled. There are number of walking tracks near the thermal pool.

The Caves and Pool are open from 10:00 am to 4:00 pm with extended hours in January. Entry fee for the caves and thermal pool: Adult - $24 & $5; Child - $5 & $2.50.

🌐 The Nut at Stanley

Located on the north west coast of Tasmania, the fishing port of Stanley is today a popular tourist destination for the for its picturesque landscape and a giant volcanic plug known as The Nut. Discovered in 1798, The Nut rises 143m and has a flat top. One can take the walking route or the chairlift to the top from where there are spectacular panoramic views across the Bass Strait and the beaches. There are a number of guided tours of the area where one can spot seals, penguins, and other wildlife. Bird watching is very popular in Stanley. Tourists also visit the neighbouring beaches in Highfield with The Nut as the

backdrop.

Recommendations for a Budget Traveller

 Accommodation

BIG4 Iluka

Reserve Road

Coles Bay 7215

Tel: 03 6257 0115

http://iluka-holiday-centre.tas.big4.com.au/

The BIG4 Iluka is located on the Freycinet National Park opposite Muirs Beach on the east coast.

It is built amidst the breathtaking natural landscape and provides the perfect getaway for the whole family. Berry farms and vineyards are also close to this accommodation that has free parking and free Wi-Fi. There is a variety of accommodations available ranging from campsites to private cabins. Rates start from $55 for a twin private ensuite.

Edgewater

4 Thomas Street

Devonport East 7310

Tel: 03 6427 8441

http://www.edgewater-devonport.com.au

This 3.5 star motel is just minutes away from the Devonport Ferry Terminal. It has 42 air-conditioned rooms in 2 categories – courtyard rooms for the budget conscious and waterfront and terrace rooms for those who want extra facilities and a view. All rooms are ensuite with Wi-Fi (surcharge) and tea/coffee facilities. The more expensive rooms come with ironing boards and a terrace. There is an onsite restaurant. Basic room rates start from $111 per night.

Hadley's Hotel

34 Murray Street

Hobart 7000

Tel: 03 6237 2999

http://hadleyshotel.com.au/

This 4-star hotel is housed in an 1834 National Listed building that was built by the convicts. It is located close to the Playhouse Theatre and the Maritime Museum. It has 71 rooms with a 24hr reception and concierge service. Parking is available for a fee but Wi-Fi is free. This smoke-free hotel has a recreation room, travel desk, and in-house bar. Rooms range from standard to suite. Basic room rates start from $130 per night.

Quality Hotel

Cnr Elizabeth Street

Hobart 7000

Tel: 03 6234 6333

Located close to the Hobart city centre, it is adjacent to the Botanical Gardens. It has free parking and a travel desk. There is an onsite restaurant and a café. There is a safe deposit facility at the reception area. The hotel serves continental breakfast. Part of the renowned Choice Hotel group, room rates of this hotel starts at $110 per night.

Edinburgh Gallery B&B

211 Macquarie Street

Hobart 7000

Tel: 03 6224 9229

http://www.artaccom.com.au

This art-filled funky boutique hotel is located close to the Hobart CBD in a historic building that has been refurbished with all modern accommodation facilities.

Airport drops and pickups can be arranged if requested.

The hotel comes with free parking, free Wi-Fi, and a

Games Room. Smoke-free rooms are available. There is

a breakfast buffet. Basic room rate starts at $89, inclusive

of breakfast.

 Places to Eat

Cornelian Bay Boathouse

Cornelian Bay

Hobart 7000

Tel: 03 622 89289

http://www.theboathouse.com.au/

Located just minutes away from the Hobart CBD, the

Boathouse restaurant is located on the bay with picture

perfect views of the waterfront and the heritage listed boatshed.

It serves all the meals from breakfast to late-hour dinner. It specializes in contemporary cuisine. Lunch menu has entrees (of beef, trout, duck) priced around $20 and main non-vegetarian dishes at $30 (vegetarian at $26). Dinner menu is priced the same with some set extra menu options.

Solo Pasta & Pizza

50b King Street

Hobart 7005

Tel: 03 6234 9898

http://solopastaandpizza.com.au/

This popular and well-rated Italian eatery at the Sandy Bay is open until late hours and also has options for delivery. It has all the usual Italian delights like the pizza, calzone, pasta, and risotto. A full meal for 2 -3 persons would cost between $12 and $20. It also serves a variety of wines and some beers.

Remi de Provence

252 Macquarie Street

Hobart 7000

Tel: 03 6223 3933

http://remideprovence.com.au/

This French restaurant has the perfect setting for a quiet and relaxed meal in a chic ambience.

There are set menus that are available for lunch and dinner that is changed from time to time. The chef hails from the French province of Provence and brings authentic French styled cooking that has made this restaurant a local favourite. A meal costs about $15 per person. There is a wide variety of wines to choose from. The restaurant also serves an exquisite array of cheese.

Stillwater River

2 Bridge Road

Launceston 7250

Tel: 03 6331 4153

http://www.stillwater.com.au/

This restaurant is open for breakfast and lunch on all 7 days and for dinner from Tuesday to Saturday. Due to the popularity of this restaurant, reservations are highly recommended. This multi award winning restaurant is the perfect place for an elegant dining experience. Dishes are typically Australian with an emphasis on fresh seafood. Main dishes are priced around $30. Set menus are available for dinner along with the a la carte menu.

AAJ Indian Café & Restaurant

146/148 Charles Street

Launceston

Tel: 03 6331 9719

http://www.aajindia.com.au/

This popular Indian restaurant with a beautiful interior décor is open for dinner from 5:00 pm until 9:30 pm. Vegetarian entrees start from $7 and the non-vegetarian from$9. Indian style grilled chicken and lamb are priced about $14. There is a limited menu of condiments and desserts priced between $5 and $7. The restaurant also serves wine, beer, spirits, and soda.

 Shopping

Island Markets

54 Gormanston Road

Hobart 7009

http://islandmarkets.com.au/

This indoor market in Moonah, Hobart, is Tasmania's largest indoor market. It is open every week from Thursday to Sunday from 9:00 am to 5:00 pm.

The Island Markets is one of the best places on the island to buy fresh produce and seafood. Between Friday and Sunday from 10:00 am until 3:00 pm, shoppers get to buy a wider variety of products including Asian groceries, plants, jewelry, handicrafts, clothing, and gift items.

Sidewalk Tribal

Castray Esplanade

Hobart 2004

http://sidewalkgallery.com.au/

Opened in the late 1980s this sidewalk gallery of African arts and crafts has become a recommended shopping attraction in Tasmania. Artworks ranging from antiques to traditional sculptures from 26 different African countries are exhibited. With real ethnic items from over 85 different

African cultures at a bargain price, the Sidewalk Tribal is a must for those who are looking for something different.

Henry Jones Design Gallery

25 Hunter Street

Hobart 7000

http://www.henryjonesdesign.com.au/

Promoting Tasmanian artists and their art, the HJD Gallery has a wide variety of artworks to choose from. The eye-catching work is featured on furniture, glass, ceramic, sculpture, and jewelry. From the quirky and funky designs to the elegant and chic, there is a wide variety to choose from.

Harvest Launceston Farmers' Market

Opposite Chancellor Hotel

Launceston

http://harvestmarket.org.au/

This market is open every Saturday from 9:30 am to 12:30 pm at the Cimitiere Street car park. This farmers' market only sells food and beverages that have been grown and produced in Tasmania. It is a great place to meet and interact with locals and get a bargain on some local favourites. Visit early in the day to avoid the rush.

Design Centre Tasmania

Tamar & Brisbane Streets

Launceston

http://www.designcentre.com.au/index.php

Located next to the car park at the corner of Tamar and Brisbane streets, this gallery and sales centre has free admission. There is a spacious exhibition hall that displays the artworks along with a small sales centre. The centre promotes contemporary art mainly featured on wood. Innovative and exquisite wooden Tasmanian art pieces at an affordable price have made the centre a favourite with its guests.

Know Before You Go

Entry Requirements

With the exception of New Zealand, nationals of most countries will need a valid passport and a visa when travelling to Australia. Upon arrival, you will also be required to fill out a passenger card, which includes a declaration regarding your health and character. A tourist visa is usually valid for 6 months, but can be extended for another 6 months. If travelling to Australia for business reasons, you will want to look into the requirements for a short term or long term business visas. The former is valid for up to 3 months, while the latter is valid for up to 4 years, but requires sponsorship from an Australian company.

Health Insurance

If visiting Australia from a country that has a reciprocal health care agreement with Australia, you will be able to use Medicare - Australia's public health insurance - for the duration of your stay. Participating countries include Ireland, New Zealand, Italy, Sweden, Norway, Slovenia, Belgium, Finland, the

Netherlands and the UK. However, this only covers emergency care and limits you to using public hospitals. Visitors on a student visa from Norway, Finland, Malta and the Republic of Ireland may require additional cover and visitors who do not have access to Medicare will be required, as part of their visa application, to obtain adequate healthcare for the duration of their stay in Australia. To extend your cover, Overseas Visitors Health Cover (OVHC) can be arranged through a number of Australian health fund companies. Additional health insurance is mandatory if visiting on a long stay working visa. There are no required vaccinations for entering Australia, but a booster shot for tetanus and diphtheria will be a good idea, if your last vaccination was more than ten years ago. If travelling from Southeast Asia, you may want to get a shot for Hepatitis A and B, as well as typhoid.

🌐 Travelling with Pets

Nearly all dogs and cats travelling to Australia will need to spend some time in quarantine, but the duration depends on the country of origin. The only countries exempt from this requirement is New Zealand, Cocos Island and Norfolk Island. The minimum quarantine period is 10 days and to qualify for this, your pet will need to be tested for rabies 6 months prior to your travel date. The cost for quarantine and customs clearance is approximately $1,800AUD. You will need to apply for an import permit for your pet. If travelling from a non-approved country such as Russia, India, Sri Lanka and the Philippines, your pet will need to spend 6 months in an approved country and be tested for rabies prior to being allowed entry in Australia. Approved countries include Antigua & Barbuda, Argentina, Austria, the Bahamas, Belgium, Bermuda, the British Virgin Islands, Brunei, Bulgaria, Canada, the Canary and Balearic Islands, the Cayman Islands, Chile, the Republic of Croatia, the Republic of Cyprus, the Czech Republic, Denmark, Finland, France, Germany, Gibraltar, Greece, Greenland, Guernsey, Hong Kong, Hungary, Ireland, the Isle of Man, Israel, Italy, Jamaica, Jersey, Kuwait, Latvia, Lithuania, Luxembourg, Macau, Malta, parts of Malaysia (Peninsular, Sabah and Sarawak only), Monaco, Montenegro, the Netherlands, Netherlands—Antilles & Aruba, Norway, Poland, Portugal, Puerto Rico, Qatar, Reunion, Saipan, Serbia, Seychelles, Slovakia, Slovenia, South Africa, South Korea, Spain, St Kitts and Nevis, St Lucia, St Vincent & the Grenadines, Sweden, Switzerland (including Liechtenstein), Taiwan, Trinidad and Tobago, the United Arab Emirates, the United Kingdom, the United States, Northern Mariana Islands, Puerto Rico and the US Virgin Islands as well as American Samoa, Bahrain, Barbados, Christmas Island, Cook Island, the

Falkland Islands, the Federated States of Micronesia, Fiji, French Polynesia, Guam, Hawaii, Iceland, Japan, Kiribati Mauritius, Nauru, New Caledonia, Niue, Palau, Papua New Guinea, Samoa, Singapore, the Solomon Islands, the Kingdom of Tonga, Tuvalu, Vanuatu and the Futuna Islands. There are quarantine stations in Sydney and Melbourne. A quarantine period can be waived in the case of service dog, provided that proper documented evidence of the dog's status is submitted, but in this case, the dog will need to be inspected upon arrival by an approved veterinarian and supervised for the 10 day period immediately after entry. You are not allowed to bring certain dog breeds such as the Dogo Argentino, Fila Brazileiro, Japanese Tosa, Pit Bull Terrier, American Pit Bull, Perro de Presa Canario or Presa Canario into Australia. Other animals that cannot be brought into Australia are chinchillas, fish, ferrets, guinea pigs, hamsters, lizards, mice, snakes, spiders and turtles. In the case of avian species, only birds originating from New Zealand are allowed.

Airports

Sydney Airport (SYD) is located just 8km south of Sydney's central business district and serves as the primary gateway for international air traffic into Australia. It is the country's busiest airport and provides connections to New Zealand, Singapore, Hong Kong, Dubai, Japan, the USA and Malaysia. Domestically, it also provides access to the country's six main states, as well as to Tasmania. The second busiest airport is **Melbourne Airport** (MEL). It is located about 23km from the central business area of Melbourne, but this is easy to reach via the Skybus Super Shuttle, which connects to the city's public transport network at the Southern Cross station. Melbourne Airport welcomes international flights from the Far East, the Middle East and the USA and also connects to Australia's top domestic destinations. The busiest airport in Queensland is **Brisbane Airport** (BNE), which provides connections to over 40 domestic destinations and over 25 international destinations. Other important airports in Queensland are the **Gold Coast Airport** (OOL) and the **Cairns Airport** (CNS). As the 4th busiest airport, **Perth Airport** (PER) serves as a gateway to Western Australia. **Adelaide Airport** (ADL) is the most important airport in the Southern Territory of Australia, while **Darwin Airport** (DRW), one of the oldest airports in Australia, opens up the Northern Territory. **Canberra Airport** (CBR) provides access to the capital. Tasmania is served by **Hobart International Airport** (HBA) in Hobart.

🌐 Airlines

Qantas Airways is the third oldest airline in the world. It was founded in 1920 through the efforts of two Australian Flying Corps veterans, W Hudson Fysh and Paul McGinness. The enterprise pioneered a series of milestones, starting with the establishment of an airmail service, the Flying Doctor Service, a regular connection between Brisbane and Darwin and the addition of international destinations such as Singapore. Qantas was an early adapter to the benefits of Boeing jumbo jets and one of the first airlines to establish a trans-Pacific route. Today it is Australia's national flag carrier and the country's largest airline. Qantas is a partner of the OneWorld Air Alliance, connecting it with British Airlines, Iberia, Japan Airlines, Finnair, LAN Airlines and Sri Lankan Airlines.

Qantas has a founding interest in Australia's budget service, Jetstar Airways, which is based at Melbourne Airport. Together with Qantas, Jetstar oversees Jetstar Asia Airways, Jetstar Pacific Airlines and Jetstar Japan. Qantas also operates a regional brand, QantasLink, which harnesses the combined coverage of Eastern Australian Airlines, Sunstate Airlines and Southern Australia Airlines to provide a regional and domestic service. Eastern Australia Airlines was founded late in the 1940s, when it served mainly to connect remote rural communities under the name Tamair. During the mid-1980s, it was acquired by Australian Airlines, who in turn sold it to Qantas in 1992.

After Qantas, Virgin Australia is the second largest airline. Founded under the Virgin brand by Richard Branson and Brett Godfrey in 2000, the company expanded rapidly after September 2001 to fill the gap left by the demise of Ansett Australia. Virgin Australia is in partnership with the regional service SkyWest Airlines as well as Air New Zealand and the US carrier Delta. Additionally, it operates the budget airline, Tigerair Australia as a subsidiary of Virgin Australia. Tigerair offers connections to 11 domestic destinations as well as nearby Bali.

West Wing Aviation is a domestic service based in Queensland and manages connections to smaller and more remote destinations within Queensland. Airnorth was founded in the late 1970s. Based in Darwin, it provides a regional service that covers the northern part of Australia. King Island Airlines offers connections between Moorabbin, near Melbourne and King Island, Tasmania.

 Hubs

Sydney Airport serves as the primary hub for Qantas Air. Qantas also uses Melbourne Airport, Brisbane Airport, Perth Airport and Adelaide Airport as hubs. Virgin Australia uses Brisbane Airport, Melbourne Airport and Sydney Airport as hubs, but also has a strong presence at Adelaide Airport, Perth Airport and Gold Coast Airport. Additionally, Melbourne Airport serves as hub for the Virgin subsidiary Tigerair, as well as Jetstar Airlines. Darwin International Airport serves as a primary hub for Airnorth. West Wing Aviation uses Townsville Airport in Queensland as hub. Brisbane Airport serves as a hub for Sunstate Airlines.

Money Matters

Currency

The currency of Australia is the Australian dollar. Notes are issued in denominations of $5, $10, $20, $50 and $100. Coins are issued in denominations of 5 cents, 10 cents, 20 cents and 50 cents as well as $1 and $2.

🌐 Banking/ATMs

ATM machines are widely distributed across Australia in both urban and rural locations. Besides bank lobbies, they are often found in shopping centers, service stations, convenience stores and pubs. You should be able to use bank cards that are part of the Cirrus, Plus or Maestro networks. Most ATMs will explicitly indicate which cards are accepted. Using a debit card is fairly easy in Australia, but many ATMs will charge an additional fee of $2 or more for non-customers. There are exceptions. As the Westpac banking group is partnered with several overseas banks including Bank of America, Scotia Bank and Barclays, customers of those banks will be exempted from the banking fee. An alternative to using your bank card is the Travelex Cash Passport, an easy-to-use prepaid card which can be topped up using your debit card.

🌐 Credit Cards

MasterCard and Visa are widely accepted throughout Australia, while Diners Club and American Express will also be legal tender at larger shops and chain stores. Some shops will decline credit cards for purchases under AUS$15 and surcharges may apply for some businesses. Until recently, credit card users in

Australia had the choice of using a PIN or signature as security for credit card transactions, but from August 2016, PIN-enabled cards will be mandatory. You should make sure that your credit card is compatible with this new policy. Also remember to advise your bank or credit card of your travel plans prior to your departure.

🌏 Tourist Tax

From July 2016, working backpackers will be taxed at 32.5 percent on their Australian income.

🌏 Claiming Back VAT

Visitors to Australia can obtain a refund on purchases of at least $300, spent at a single business. Residents of the Australia's External Territories - the Norfolk Islands, Christmas Island and the Cocos (Keeling) Islands - also qualify for a refund from GST paid under the Tourist Refund Scheme (TRS). To obtain a refund, you must present valid documentation of your purchases in the form of a tax invoice or sales receipt at an international airport or seaport when departing Australia and this should happen within 60 days of making those purchases. You should keep the goods handy within your hand luggage, to have it available for inspection. To save time, download the TRS app where you can enter details electronically and use a specially dedicated shortcut queue to process your claim.

🌐 Tipping Policy

In Australia, restaurants are required by law to pay their waiting staff a working wage and tipping is not really expected, although the influence of tourism as well as American culture has influenced Australian attitudes in recent years. In high-end restaurants, roughly half of the diners might be expected to leave a tip and in big cities, it will be more common to tip. If service is good and you want to show your appreciation, 10 percent is regarded as fair and sufficient. It is not common practice to tip in hotels and in casinos, tipping is forbidden. In bars, it is accepted practice to tell the bartender to keep the change. The same applies to cab drivers.

 Connectivity

Mobile Phones

Australia uses the GSM mobile network, which means that it should be compatible with phones from the UK or the European Union, but may be incompatible with phones from the USA and Canada. If you are able to use Australian networks, you will still face the high charges levied for international roaming. There is an alternative. If your phone is unlocked, you will be able to replace your own SIM card with an Australian SIM card for the duration of your stay.

Australia has 3 basic mobile networks - Telstra, Vodafone and Optus. Telstra offers the best coverage of Australia's rural and more remote locations, but is also one of the more expensive operators. If you plan to stick to urban locations, the coverage offered by Optus and Vodafone might be sufficient for your needs. Telstra sim cards are available at $2, with recharge packages starting at $20. Data only packages are priced at between $30 and $50. Optus sim cards begin at $2 for just the sim, with top-ups priced at between $10 and $50. Vodafone pre-paid sim cards begin at $1 for just the sim, with data packages priced at between $3 and $15. For a super budget option, consider the deals offered by the reseller Amaysim, which also offers the option to pay for top-ups online, via PayPal.

⊕ Dialling Code

The dialling code for Australia is +61.

⊕ Emergency Numbers

General emergency: 000

Text Emergency Relay Service: 106

MasterCard: 1800 120 113

Visa: 1800 450 346

⊕ General Information

⊕ Public Holidays

1 January: New Year's Day

26 January: Australia Day

March/April: Good Friday

March/April: Easter Monday

25 April: Anzac Day

23 June: The Queen's Birthday

25 December: Christmas

26 December: Boxing Day

There are various holidays that are celebrated at state level or within certain religious communities.

🌐 Time Zones

The Australian continent is divided into three different time zones. The eastern states of Queensland, Victoria and New South Wales, as well as the Australian Capital Territory and Tasmania fall under Australian East Standard Time (AEST), which can be calculated as Greenwich Mean Time/Co-ordinated Universal Time (GMT/UTC) +10. Australian Central Standard Time (ACST) is used in the Northern Territory, South Australia and in the town of Broken Hill, which is found in the western part of New South Wales. Australian Central Standard Time can be calculated as Greenwich Mean Time/Co-ordinated Universal Time (GMT/UTC) +9 and a half hour. Western Australia uses Australian Western Standard time, which can be calculated as Greenwich Mean Time/Co-ordinated Universal Time (GMT/UTC) +8.

🌏 Daylight Savings Time

For Daylight Savings Time, clocks are set forward by one hour at 2am on the first Sunday in October and set back one hour at 3am on the first Sunday in April. Queensland, Western Australia and the Northern Territory do not observe Daylight Savings Time.

🌏 School Holidays

In Australia, the academic year runs from January to December. Generally, schools open towards the end of January or very early in February. There is a 2 to 3 week break from the end of March or early in April, a winter vacation in June/July and a 2 week spring break in September or October. The summer vacation is usually from mid December to the end of January. Exact dates are set by the state authority in question and may vary.

🌏 Trading Hours

Trading hours are set at state rather than national level, but in most states there are little or no restrictions on hours. Generally, shopping hours in Australia are from 8am to 9pm on weekdays, 8am to 5.30pm on Saturdays and 9am to 6pm on Sundays. Most non-essential businesses will be closed on ANZAC Day, Good Friday and Christmas Day. In South Australia, trade on Sundays and Public Holidays are restricted to the hours between 11am and 5pm. In Queensland, most shopping centers close at 5pm, but will stay open for late trade on one day of the week. In Western Australia, large businesses and chain stores are restricted to trading between 9am and 5pm from Monday to Saturday and between 11am and 5pm on Sundays and Public Holidays.

🌏 Driving Policy

Australians drive on the left hand side of the road. In most states, you will be able to drive on a foreign licence, provided that it is valid and that an English translation (or International Driver's Licence) is available. The minimum driving age varies from 16 years and 6 months in the Northern Territory to 18 in Victoria, but in most states it is 17 years. The speed limit is

60km per hour for cities and urban areas, 50km per hour in suburban areas and 110km per hour on highways and rural roads. Laws regarding texting and the use of cell phones while driving vary, but in most states, a hands-free kit is required. Learner drivers or inexperienced drivers are not allowed to handle their phones at all while driving. The legal limit for drinking and driving is a Blood Alcohol Concentration (BAC) of 0.05%, but learner drivers and inexperienced drivers are not allowed to drink at all when driving.

🌐 Drinking Policy

In Australia, the minimum drinking age is 18. Children under the age of 18 are only allowed on licenced premises, if accompanied by a parent. Only businesses with a liquor licence are allowed to supply alcohol to the public and by law, they are required to ask customers and patrons for some form of identification. Local councils in Australia have the power to declare an area a dry zone, which means that no alcohol may be consumed there. The ban may relate to a particular event or can apply on an ongoing basis.

Smoking Policy

In the early 1990s, Australia introduced legislation to restrict smoking in public places. Smoking is banned in restaurants, bars and licenced clubs, although there are designated smoking areas. Recently, the ban was widened to include smoking in vehicles with children under the age of 18. Smoking is also forbidden in outdoor play areas for children, at swimming pools, bus stops and railway stations. In New South Wales, you may not smoke within 4m of a building entrance and in Western Australia, smoking is prohibited in the patrolled areas of beaches. All tobacco products are required by law to carry health warnings.

Electricity

Electricity: 230 volts

Frequency: 50 Hz

Australia's electricity sockets are compatible with the Type I plugs, a plug that features three rectangular pins or prongs, arranged in a triangular shape, with two of the pins set at opposing angles to each other. They are similar to the plugs and sockets used in Fiji. If travelling from the USA or Canada, you will also need a power converter or transformer to convert the voltage from 230 to 110, to avoid damage to your appliances. The latest models of certain types of camcorders, cell phones and digital cameras are dual-voltage, which means that they were manufactured with a built in converter, but you will have to consult your electronics dealer about that.

🌏 Food & Drink

When they have the time for a hearty breakfast, Australians love a fry-up similar to the full English breakfast with eggs, bacon, sausage, mushroom and baked beans. Other popular breakfast options include porridge, cereal and milk or simply a slice of toast with vegemite - that is Australia's twist on good old Marmite. Technically, Australia lies in the Orient and a robust community of Asian immigrants has ensured the enduring popularity of Asian cuisine. Australia also sometimes offers exotic game, in the form of kangaroo, emu and crocodile steak. Adventurous diners will want to sample bush food, but it is not for the faint of heart. Bush tucker originated with the hunter-gatherer lifestyle of Australia's Aboriginal people and incorporates a variety of home-grown fruits and vegetables, as well as edible seeds and insects. One of the best known delicacies is the witchetty grub, which can be eaten raw or cooked. Other indigenous staples include bush yam, bush banana, conkleberries and wattle seeds.

In Australia, beer is serious business, complete with its own lingo of buzz phrases. Australians refer to a can as a "tinnie", a case of 24 cans as a "slab" and a bottle of beer as a "brownie" or, in the case of a long-necked bottle, as a "tally". While a short-necked bottle is called a "stubby", do not mistake it with a "Darwin stubby", the Northern Territory variety with a 2.25 litre capacity. Even glasses are divided into "pints", "schooners", "middys" or "pots", according to size, and you should say "My shout" to announce your intention to buy the next round.

The most popular beer brands in Australia are VB (Victoria Bitter) and Castlemaine's XXXX Gold and other beers worth sampling include Carlton Draught, Toohey's Extra Dry, Hahn Premium Light, Crown Lager, Pure Blonde and James Boag's Premium. In Queensland and New South Wales, Bundeberg beer is another favorite. Australia has a robust wine industry, of which the best known export is Penfolds Grange. Other well established wineries are Wolf Blass, Lindemans, Rosemount, Jacob's Creek, Yalumba, Berri Estates, Yellowglen and Hardy Wine Co. Tasmania produces top notch whiskies, such as the award-winning Sullivan's Cove and great cider, such as Red

Sails, Lost Pippin and Pagan Cider. When it comes to soft drinks, Coca-Cola rules. Australia's taste for coffee has been influenced by the significant community of Italian immigrants. Visiting techno-geeks can try the newly launched Smartcup, an Australian invention which can be linked to a CafePay app and lets you pay for your daily brew online.

🌐 Useful Websites

http://www.australia.com/en

http://wikitravel.org/en/Australia

https://www.australianexplorer.com/

http://www.downundr.com/tips-and-tricks/top-ten-destinations

http://www.britz.com.au/

http://www.driveaustralia.com.au/suggested-routes/

http://ozyroadtripper.com.au/

http://australiaroadtrip.co.uk/

https://www.ozexperience.com/

Printed in Great Britain
by Amazon

20754419R00050